Piano · Vocal · Guitar

JOHN LEGEND
DARKNESS AND

2 I KNOW BETTER

7 PENTHOUSE FLOOR

15 DARKNESS AND LIGHT

19 OVERLOAD

25 LOVE ME NOW

32 WHAT YOU DO TO ME

39 SUREFIRE

46 RIGHT BY YOU

52 TEMPORARILY PAINLESS

58 HOW CAN I BLAME YOU

63 SAME OLD STORY

67 MARCHING INTO THE DARK

ISBN 978-1-4950-8946-6

HAL•LEONARD®

7777 W. BLUEMOUND RD. P.O. BOX 13819 MILWAUKEE, WI 53213

In Australia Contact:
Hal Leonard Australia Pty. Ltd.
4 Lentara Court
Cheltenham, Victoria, 3192 Australia
Email: ausadmin@halleonard.com.au

Visit Hal Leonard Online at
www.halleonard.com

I KNOW BETTER

Words and Music by JOHN STEPHENS,
BLAKE MILLS and WILL OLDHAM

They say, "Sing ___ what you know," ___ but I've sung what they want. ___ Some folks do ___
in my past, ___ things no one can be proud of. ___ But I stand in the

what they're told; ___ but ba - by, this time I won't. ___ When I
light I've cast, ___ and turn a - way from an - y lack of love. ___ Oh, ___ when I

look through that ___ door, ___ I know the truth from lie. ___ Some
walk through that ___ door, ___ I say, ___ "Here I go." ___ You see

PENTHOUSE FLOOR

Words and Music by JOHN STEPHENS,
BLAKE MILLS, GREG KURSTIN
and CHANCELLOR BENNETT

Additional Lyrics

(Spoken:) I heard this old joke once, it was like, uh...

Knock knock. Who there? It's us. Us who?
Just us. Who dis? Just playin'. Just me.
New phone, new hair, new era.
(Sung:) I'm in the penthouse, baby.

(Spoken:) Handpicked from bad apples and bad eggs.
Held back, I had to grab crab legs.
And then there were only but a few.
Conversations held with patience; what a party, what a view!

What a dress! What a song!
What a beautiful time!
My folks downstairs still waitin' in line.
They never been in these rooms, never stayed with these folks,
Never laughed at the news, never hated these jokes.

So was I a fly in my soup? In a group, undercover.
Forcing a new smile, he tells me another.
He said, "What happened to the boy that climbed up the trunk?"
Then he pushed me off the top and said, "Jump, nigga, jump!"

DARKNESS AND LIGHT

Words and Music by JOHN STEPHENS,
JOHN HENRY RYAN and WILL OLDHAM

OVERLOAD

Words and Music by JOHN STEPHENS,
BLAKE MILLS and MIGUEL PIMENTEL

LOVE ME NOW

Words and Music by JOHN STEPHENS,
JOHN HENRY RYAN and BLAKE MILLS

WHAT YOU DO TO ME

Words and Music by JOHN STEPHENS,
BLAKE MILLS, MATT SWEENEY, JULIA MICHAELS,
JUSTIN TRANTER and MICHAEL TUCKER

That's what you do to me. (That's what you do to me.) That's what you do to me. (That's what you do to me.) That's what you do, you al - ways do me right, ___ scream - ing through the night, ___ make me love and hate you at the same time. _ That's what you do to me.

SUREFIRE

Words and Music by JOHN STEPHENS,
BLAKE MILLS, WILL OLDHAM, JUSTIN TRANTER,
LUDWIG GORANSSON and JULIA MICHAELS

love, __ but it's al - right. __ I may not know __ a lot of things, but __

__ I know __ that we're sure - fi - re, __

yeah, know __ that we're sure - fi -

- re. __ Eh.

D.S. al Coda

RIGHT BY YOU
(For Luna)

Words and Music by JOHN STEPHENS,
BLAKE MILLS and ETHAN GRUSKA

TEMPORARILY PAINLESS

Words and Music by JOHN STEPHENS,
JOHN HENRY RYAN and BLAKE MILLS

* Recorded a half step lower.

HOW CAN I BLAME YOU

Words and Music by JOHN STEPHENS,
BLAKE MILLS, MATTHEW SWEENEY
and FRANCIS WHITE

SAME OLD STORY

Words and Music by JOHN STEPHENS,
BLAKE MILLS and TOBIAS JESSO JR.

Recorded a half step higher.

MARCHING INTO THE DARK

Words and Music by JOHN STEPHENS,
BLAKE MILLS and TOBIAS JESSO JR.